First Facts™

The Senses

Seeing

by Rebecca Olien

Consultant:
Eric H. Chudler, PhD, Research Associate Professor
Department of Anesthesiology, University of Washington
Seattle, Washington

Capstone
press
Mankato, Minnesota

First Facts is published by Capstone Press,
151 Good Counsel Drive, P.O. Box 669, Mankato, Minnesota 56002.
www.capstonepress.com

Library of Congress Cataloging-in-Publication Data
Olien, Rebecca.
   Seeing / by Rebecca Olien.
   p. cm.—(First facts. The senses)
   Summary: "Explains the sense of sight and how the eyes work as sense organs"—Provided by publisher.
   Includes bibliographical references and index.
   ISBN 0-7368-4302-7 (hardcover)
   1. Vision—Juvenile literature. I. Title. II. Series.
QP475.7.O455 2006
612.8'4—dc22   2004027221

Editorial Credits
Wendy Dieker, editor; Juliette Peters, designer; Wanda Winch, photo researcher/photo editor

Photo Credits
Brand X Pictures/Burke/Triolio Productions, cover (net)
Bruce Coleman Inc./Kim Taylor, cover (butterfly)
Capstone Press/Karon Dubke, cover (girl), 1 (girl), 8, 9, 14, 15 (boy), 17, 21
Corbis/Royalty-Free, 15 (background)
Digital Vision, 13; Gerry Ellis and Michael Durham, 19
Gem Photo Studio/Dan Delaney, 16
Getty Images Inc./Arthur Tilley, 6–7; Seth Kushner, 5
Juliette Peters, 12
Photodisc/Siede Preis, 1 (butterfly)
Wildlife of Wisconsin/Susan Theys, 20

1 2 3 4 5 6 10 09 08 07 06 05

Table of Contents

The Sense of Seeing

We use our five senses to learn about the world around us. We can touch, smell, hear, taste, and see things. Some of our body parts send messages to the brain. The brain uses the messages to react to the world. Eyes are body parts that send messages about what we see.

Fun Fact!

Eyeball is a good name for the eye. Eyeballs are round like balls. Our eyelids make them look like ovals.

5

How You See

To see, you need light. Light bounces off objects and into your eyes. Light reflects off a bug and enters your eyes. Eyes send messages to your brain about the bug. The brain tells you about the shape, size, and color of the bug.

Fun Fact!
People cannot see color in low light. In a dark room, colorful objects look gray or black.

The Eyes

Eyes collect light. Light travels through the eye's clear outer covering called the **cornea**. The light then goes through a hole called the **pupil**.

cornea

pupil

iris

The **iris** controls how much light
goes into the pupil. This colored muscle
changes the pupil's size. A large pupil
lets in more light than a small pupil.

Inside the Eye

Light that enters the eye passes through the pupil to the **lens**. The lens bends the light onto the back of the eye. This area is the **retina**.

The retina sends information to the **optic nerve**. The optic nerve sends messages to the brain. The brain tells you what you see.

Fun Fact!

The lens turns what you see upside down. Your brain has to flip the messages coming from the retina.

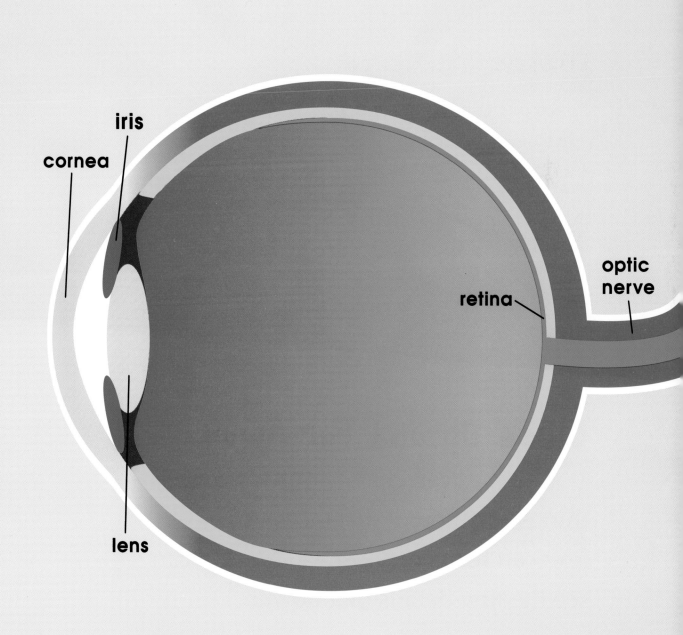

cornea

iris

lens

retina

optic nerve

11

Close Up and Far Away

The eyes can change quickly to see things at different distances. An eye's lens can **focus** on close objects. We can see the tiny details of a flower.

Then, the lens quickly changes
shape to see things far away. We
can clearly see faraway mountains.

Taking Care of the Eyes

Eyes are easily hurt. Protect your eyes so they don't get hurt or scratched. Wear safety glasses when working with sharp objects.

Sunglasses protect your eyes
from strong light. Bright sunlight can
damage the eyes. Never look directly at
the sun, even while wearing sunglasses.

Loss of Sight

Some people have poor eyesight. Many of them wear eyeglasses to improve their sight.

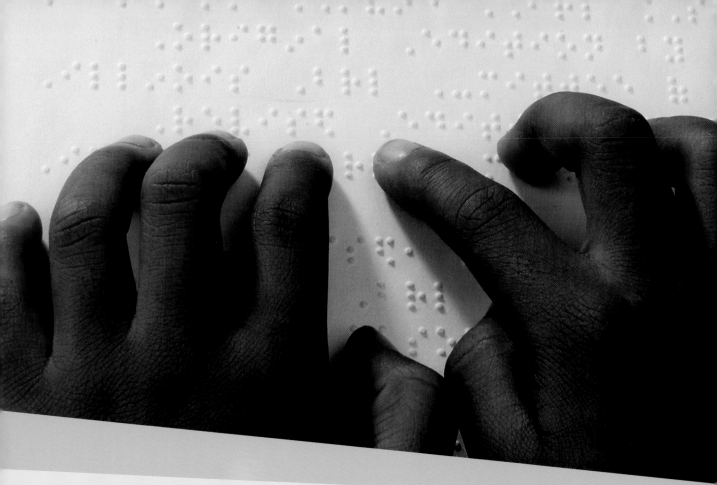

People can lose their sight from
injury, disease, or problems before birth.
People who are blind use braille to read
with their fingers.

Dragonfly Eyes

The dragonfly has good eyesight. This insect's big eyes wrap around its head. It can see in many directions. The dragonfly has 28,000 lenses in each eye. Good eyesight helps the dragonfly catch small flying insects.

Fun Fact!

A dragonfly's good eyesight helps it fly fast and change directions quickly.

Amazing but True!

A great horned owl named Minerva was given back her sight. She couldn't hunt because she couldn't see. A doctor gave her new lenses. Minerva then returned to the wild. She is the first wild animal in the world to have artificial lenses.

Hands On: Pupil Peeking

Your eye's pupil is actually a hole. It is black because the inside of your eye is dark. The ring around your pupil is the iris. This muscle changes the size of the pupil. In this experiment, you can watch your eyes at work.

What You Need

hand-held mirror

What You Do

1. Look into your eyes in the mirror. Look closely at your pupil and iris. How big is your pupil?
2. Go into a darker room. If you need to, cover the windows to make the room dark. Close your eyes for a few seconds.
3. Open your eyes and look into the mirror. How big are your pupils? What does your iris look like?
4. Now turn on the lights. Look in the mirror and watch your iris work. Did your pupils change size?

Pupils get larger in the dark to let in more light. Pupils get smaller in bright light, so less light enters your eyes.

Glossary

cornea (KOR-nee-uh)—a clear layer covering parts of the eye

focus (FOH-kuhss)—to adjust to see something clearly

iris (EYE-riss)—the colored muscle that controls the size of the pupil

lens (LENZ)—something that bends light to focus sight; eyes have lenses to bend light onto the retina.

optic nerve (OP-tik NURV)—a thin fiber that sends messages from the eye to the brain

pupil (PYOO-puhl)—the hole in the center of the eye that lets in light

retina (RET-uhn-uh)—the lining inside the back of the eyeball

Read More

Levine, Shar, and Leslie Johnstone. *Super Senses.* First Science Experiments. New York: Sterling Publishing, 2003.

Simon, Seymour. *Eyes and Ears.* New York: HarperCollins, 2003.

Ziefert, Harriet. *You Can't Taste a Pickle with Your Ear: A Book About Your 5 Senses.* Brooklyn, N.Y.: Blue Apple Books, 2002.

Internet Sites

FactHound offers a safe, fun way to find Internet sites related to this book. All of the sites on FactHound have been researched by our staff.

Here's how:

1. Visit *www.facthound.com*
2. Type in this special code **0736843027** for age-appropriate sites. Or enter a search word related to this book for a more general search.
3. Click on the **Fetch It** button.

FactHound will fetch the best sites for you!

Index